TIME FOR KIDS
BOOK OF WHY

STELLAR
SPACE

TIME For Kids

Managing Editor: Nellie Gonzalez Cutler
Editor: Brenda Iasevoli
Creative Director: Jennifer Kraemer-Smith

Time Home Entertainment

Publisher: Jim Childs
Vice President, Brand &
Digital Strategy: Steven Sandonato
Executive Director, Marketing Services: Carol Pittard
Executive Director, Retail & Special Sales: Tom Mifsud
Executive Publishing Director: Joy Bomba
Director, Bookazine Development
& Marketing: Laura Adam
Vice President, Finance Director: Vandana Patel
Publishing Director: Megan Pearlman
Assistant General Counsel: Simone Procas
Assistant Director, Special Sales: Ilene Schreider
Brand Manager: Jonathan White
Associate Prepress Manager: Alex Voznesenskiy
Associate Production Manager: Kimberly Marshall
Associate Project Manager: Stephanie Braga

Editorial Director: Stephen Koepp
Senior Editor: Roe D'Angelo
Copy Chief: Rina Bander
Design Manager: Anne-Michelle Gallero
Editorial Operations: Gina Scauzillo

Special thanks: Katherine Barnet, Brad Beatson, Jeremy Biloon, Susan Chodakiewicz, Rose Cirrincione, Assu Etsubneh, Mariana Evans, Christine Font, Susan Hettleman, Hillary Hirsch, David Kahn, Amy Mangus, Nina Mistry, Dave Rozzelle, Ricardo Santiago, Adriana Tierno

Copyright © 2010 Time for Kids Big Book of WHY
Copyright © 2014 Time Home Entertainment Inc.
All TIME FOR KIDS material © 2014 by Time Inc.
TIME FOR KIDS and the red border design are registered trademarks of Time Inc.

Contents of this book previously appeared in Time For Kids Big Book of WHY.

For information on TIME FOR KIDS magazine for the classroom or home, go to TIMEFORKIDS.COM or call 1-800-777-8600.
For subscriptions to SI KIDS, go to SIKIDS.COM or call 1-800-889-6007.

Published by TIME FOR KIDS Books,
An imprint of Time Home Entertainment Inc.
135 West 50th Street
New York, NY 10020

ISBN 10: 1-60320-985-9
ISBN 13: 978-1-60320-985-4

TIME FOR KIDS is a trademark of Time Inc.

We welcome your comments and suggestions about TIME FOR KIDS Books. Please write to us at:
TIME FOR KIDS Books, Attention: Book Editors,
P.O. Box 11016, Des Moines, IA 50336-1016
If you would like to order any of our hardcover Collector's Edition books, please call us at1-800-327-6388 (Monday through Friday, 7 a.m. to 8 p.m., or Saturday, 7 a.m. to 6 p.m., Central Time).

1 QGT 14

Picture credits
t = top, b = bottom, c = center,
r = right, l = left

Front and Back cover:
Astronomical Celestial Map:
ARCHITECTEUR, shutterstock.com
Astronaut: lculig, shutterstock.com
Asteroid: MarcelClemens,
shutterstock.com
Satellite: Yurij, shutterstock.com
Radio Telescope: lexaarts,
shutterstock.com
Planet: italianphoto, hutterstock.com
Moon: NataliSuns, shutterstock.com
Diamonds: alexRem, shutterstock.com
Sputnik: FreshPaint, shutterstock.com

Contents Page:
Lick Observatory, Marshall Space Flight Center, Martin D. Vonka/Shutterstock, Wojciech Zwierzynski/Istockphoto
Inside:
Bigstock: Zastol'skiy: 5, Anthony Mattucci: 15b.
Dreamstime: Francisco Caravana: 9t.
Dannyphoto: 25t, Kutt Niinepuu: 43b.
Fotolia: Fred: 39l.
Glow Images: SuperStock: 34.
Istockphoto: Bart Van Den Dikkenberg: 8b, Wojciech Zwierzynski: 18t, Sven Herrmann: 35b, Lutherhill: 42tl, Christopher Bernard: 45b.

Library of Congress Prints and Photographs Division, Washington, D.C.: 35t, 37t, 41t, 41b.
NASA: 4t, GSFC/LaRC/JPL, MISR Team: 6t, 11b, 17t, 48, Goddard Space Flight Center: 20t, 20b, Kennedy Space Center: 21l, 21r, JAXA: 22t, JPL-Caltech: 22b, Lick Observatory: 23t, 23b, 24t, The Hubble Heritage/STScI/AURA: 24bl, JPL-Caltech: 26, Hubble Space Telescope: 27t, JPL/Space Science Institute: 27b, 28t, Marshall Space Flight Center: 28b, Johns Hopkins University Applied Physics Laboratory/Southwest Research Institute: 29, CXC/JPL-Caltech/CfA: 30t, ESA/HEIC and The Hubble Heritage Team (STScI/

AURA: 30b, 31t, 31b, JPL-Caltech: 32t, 47, Marshall Space Flight Center: 32b, Jet Propulsion Laboratory: 34b.
National Oceanic and Atmospheric Administration: 17b.
Photolibrary: Oxford Scientific (OSF): 4b, Fogstock LLC: 6b, Jacob Hutchings: 15t, Mary Evans Picture Library: 24br, Peter Arnold Images: 34t, Patrick Strattner: 40t.
Shutterstock: Juliengrondin: 7l, Bychkov Kirill Alexandrovich: 7r, Ibird: 8t, Rovenko Design: 9b, Shuttertsock: 10t, Juliengrondin: 10b, Jan Martin Will: 11t, Lee Prince: 12t, Christina Richards: 12b, Epic Stock: 13, Shutterstock: 14t, Adisa: 14b, Hank Shiffman: 15t, Ivan

Cholakov Gostock-dot-net: 16, Jan Martin Will: 18b, Alexander Maksimov, Stukkey, Patricia Hofmeester, Zentilia: 19, Igor Golovniov: 25b, Nikm: 33t, Fesus Robert: 33b, Maggee: 36t, Jack F, Aaron Amat: 36b, Maxim Petrichuk: 37b, Perkus: 38t, Lisa F. Young: 38b, Pavel Shchegolev: 39r, Losevsky Pavel: 40b, Martin D. Vonka: 42tr, Monkey Business Images: 42b, Gelpi: 44t, Studio Foxy: 44c, Melinda Fawver: 44b, Ragnarock: 45t.
Q2AMedia Art Bank: 10, 37, 38.

CONTENTS & QUESTIONS

Here's a look at some of the questions inside.

Why is Earth so different from other planets?

Unlike other planets in our solar system, Earth is home to an amazing variety of living things. Earth is just the right distance from the sun to allow water, oxygen, and other building blocks of life to form. The planet is also protected by an atmosphere—layers of gases that shield us from being harmed by the sun's powerful rays.

How did life form on Earth?

WHY DO SOME CREATURES LIVE IN UNUSUAL PLACES?

There are some wacky places on Earth where creatures live. Organisms called extremophiles have adapted to life in places we might think are uninhabitable. These extremophiles live deep in the ocean where it is very dark and cold, or in the acidic waters of Yellowstone National Park.

Scientists study extremophiles to see what life might be like on Mar

How do tornadoes form?

A tornado is a column of rapidly rotating air that generally begins life as a thunderstorm. The atmosphere becomes unstable when warm, moist air bangs into a wall of cool, dry air. Near the ground sits a layer of warm, humid air. In the upper atmosphere is a layer of cold air. The warm air rises. The cold air falls. A tornado is born when the wind's speed and direction causes the rising air to rotate vertically in the middle of the storm.

WHY DOES TORNADO ALLEY GET MORE TORNADOES THAN OTHER PLACES?

Tornado Alley is a part of the United States stretching from Texas to North Dakota. Although tornadoes occur throughout the U.S., they take place more often and with more force in Tornado Alley. Why is that? Tornado Alley is flat. It is also where warm, moist air from the Gulf of Mexico and cold, dry air from Canada collide. When that happens, tornadoes are born.

WHY ARE TORNADOES DANGEROUS?

Tornadoes are storms of swirling wind that are among the most violent in nature. Tornadoes can generate wind speeds of 250 mph (402.34 km) or more. As they move, tornadoes can sometimes cut a path of destruction a mile wide and more than 50 miles (80 km) long. Once, a tornado picked up a motel sign in Oklahoma and dropped it 30 miles (48 km) away in Arkansas.

Why can astronauts see the Grand Canyon from space?

The Grand Canyon is more than a big hole in the ground. It is a wonder of nature. The canyon is 277 miles (445.8 km) long, up to 18 miles (29 km) wide, and one mile (1.6 km) deep. Along with other forces, the rushing water of the Colorado River carved out the canyon over millions of years. The Grand Canyon is so huge that astronauts can see it from space without a telescope.

WHY DOES THE GRAND CANYON GET SO COLD AT NIGHT?

The Grand Canyon is in the desert. During a summer day, the bottom of the canyon can get extremely hot, with temperatures reaching more than 100°F (38°C). Deserts have very dry air that holds little moisture and heat. As soon as the sun sets, the air cools, especially at the rim of the canyon, causing a big temperature change.

Why is the Grand Canyon colorful?

The Grand Canyon looks as if someone piled up layers of colorful rock. As the rocks eroded over thousands and thousands of years, the minerals in the rocks created different colors, including reds, browns, and oranges.

Lava can get as hot as 2,000°F (1,100°C).

WHY DO PEOPLE GET SICK WHEN A VOLCANO ERUPTS?

A volcano's ash and dust can cause breathing problems. Volcanoes also spew poison gas into the air. The Kilauea volcano in Hawaii vents about 1,800 tons (1,632.93 MT) of sulfur dioxide a day. The ash and dust can harm drinking water, and create volcanic smog called "vog" that makes it hard to see.

How does a volcano work?

Think of a volcano as a soda can. Shake the can, and gas and pressure build up inside. Open the top and—*bam!*—an explosion occurs. Volcanoes work much the same way. The heat deep inside Earth is so intense that it melts rock and creates explosive gases. Scientists call that molten rock magma. Magma slowly rises to the surface, collecting in underground chambers. Eventually, the pressure of the magma becomes so great that it pushes through Earth's crust. Soon a volcano is blowing its top.

WHY SHOULDN'T I TOUCH LAVA?

Lava is just another name for magma that reaches the surface of the Earth. If you find yourself close enough to a volcano that you can touch the lava, run as fast as you can! Lava is hot, hot, hot! How hot? It can reach temperatures of 2,000°F (1,100°C). A volcano can shoot lava into the air up to 2,000 feet (609.6 m).

Why do **earthquakes destroy** some **buildings** and not others?

During an earthquake, the ground shakes, twists, and heaves, causing buildings to move. Houses can shift on their foundations, crack, and tumble to the ground. Some buildings, however, are built to withstand violent earthquakes. Some are also braced with special materials to keep them standing.

How do tectonic plates move?

Earth's outermost layer is separated into a dozen or so tectonic plates, enormous slabs of Earth's crust that slowly move across the surface of the planet. The plates move by riding on top of the Earth's hot **mantle**. The tectonic plate movement varies from 4 to 6 inches (0.10 to 0.15 m) per year.

This crack was caused by an earthquake.

WHY CAN I FLOAT IN THE OCEAN?

Salt in the ocean makes the water denser, or thicker. The denser the water, the easier it is to float on it.

Why is the ocean salty?

A Norwegian folktale says ocean water is salty because a mill at the bottom of the ocean is grinding out salt. The truth is the ocean gets its salt from rocks on land. When rain falls, it erodes the rocks. The water dissolves minerals from the rocks, including chloride and sodium (the main ingredients in salt). Those minerals flow down streams and rivers into the ocean.

Why shouldn't I drink seawater?

First, it tastes yucky. Second, it causes **dehydration**. If you drink salt- water, your body will have to get rid of more water than you drank in order to push out the extra salt. As a result, you will be thirstier than you were before.

Why is the ozone layer important?

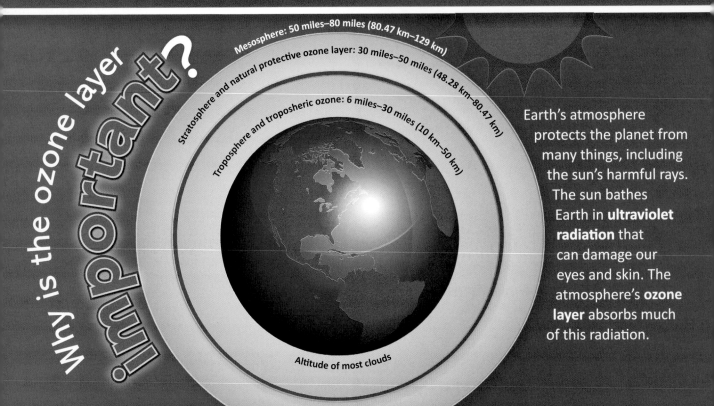

Mesosphere: 50 miles–80 miles (80.47 km–129 km)

Stratosphere and natural protective ozone layer: 30 miles–50 miles (48.28 km–80.47 km)

Troposphere and troposheric ozone: 6 miles–30 miles (10 km–50 km)

Altitude of most clouds

Earth's atmosphere protects the planet from many things, including the sun's harmful rays. The sun bathes Earth in **ultraviolet radiation** that can damage our eyes and skin. The atmosphere's **ozone layer** absorbs much of this radiation.

Why does the atmosphere "breathe"?

Just like us, the atmosphere needs to breathe every once in a while. Scientists discovered in 2008 that Earth's atmosphere expands and contracts every nine days or so—in other words, it breathes. They say the solar wind, highly charged atomic particles produced by the sun, causes the atmosphere to expand and contract.

WHY IS IT MORE DIFFICULT TO BREATHE AT HIGHER ALTITUDES?

At high altitudes, 1 mile (1.61 km) or more above sea level, the air is thinner. That doesn't mean the air is actually thin. It means there's less oxygen available at that height. Air pressure decreases the higher you go. For your lungs to fill with air, the air pressure in your lungs should be less than the pressure of the air outside. Otherwise, breathing becomes difficult.

Why don't you feel upside down in Antarctica?

Relative to the rest of the world, people and penguins in Antarctica are upside down. In fact, people living in New York and London walk around in a tilted position, while people on the equator stand sideways. Still, we all feel as though we are standing straight up. Why is that? Earth's **gravity** pulls us toward Earth's center. If the world were flat, we would all experience the same "downward" direction. Since Earth is a sphere, Earth's center is straight down from wherever you are standing. So, people are tilted or upside down with respect to each other, even though they think they are upright.

Why don't we fall off the planet?

There are many forces that want to fling us into outer space. The gravitational force of the moon tries to pull us off the planet, as does Earth spinning on its axis. Yet, gravity is always pulling us toward the center of the Earth. Earth's gravity is so strong that it keeps our feet on the ground.

Earth's gravity causes quakes on asteroids that are passing 30 million miles (48.3 million km) away.

WHY DOESN'T EARTH FLY OFF INTO SPACE?

Once again, gravity saves the day. This time, though, it is the sun's gravitational tug, and the gravitational pull from the other planets, that keeps Earth anchored in its orbit.

Why is air in spray cans cold?

People use canned air to clean dust from computer keyboards, cameras, and other items. Canned air is not the same as the air you breathe. Canned air is usually a combination of nitrogen and other gases. When a gas is placed under a high amount of pressure and then released, there is a tremendous drop in temperature. The surrounding air and the can itself get cold as the gas expands outward. Don't spray canned air on your skin. You might get frostbite. Always use canned air with a parent's okay.

Why can't we see air?

Air is all around us, but we can't see it. That's because Earth's atmosphere is made up of several gases, including oxygen, water vapor, and carbon dioxide. The molecules of these gases don't absorb light that our eyes can see, so air is invisible to us.

WHY DOES HOT AIR CAUSE A BALLOON TO RISE?

When air is heated, its molecules move faster. The faster the molecules move, the more space they take up. Because hot air is less dense than cold air, the hot air "floats" on top of the cold air, causing the balloon to rise. When the air inside the balloon cools, the balloon goes down.

Why does the ocean have waves?

Have you ever tried to catch a wave? It's pretty hard. Winds create waves on oceans and lakes. When the wind blows, it transfers some of its energy to the water. **Friction** between the air molecules and water molecules creates a wave.

HOW DO TIDES FORM?

Tides form when the moon's gravitational pull tugs on Earth's oceans. When that happens, the sea rises toward the moon. High tides occur on the side of the Earth facing the moon. Low tides occur on the side of Earth facing away from the moon.

Why are tsunamis so **dangerous**?

Tsunamis are monster ocean waves caused by underwater earthquakes, volcanic eruptions, or landslides. The energy created by these geological disturbances spreads outward from the **epicenter**. Large volumes of water, known as swells, also move from the center. The swells become high waves as they bunch up in shallow water near the shore. By that time the monster wave might have grown as high as 164 feet (50 m) or more.

Why isn't the sky black, purple, or green?

WHY DO CLOUDS FLOAT?

Clouds float because the cloud is warmer than the air around it.

It might be cool to have a green sky for a day or two, but don't count on that happening. During a clear day, the sky is blue. Why is that? Light from the sun, which is made up of different rainbow colors, has to pass through atoms of nitrogen and oxygen in the atmosphere. Because those atoms are so tiny, they cause light to break up. The atoms break up the color blue much more easily than they do other colors.

Why do clouds look like animals?

Some clouds look like animals. Others look like people. Some even look like old cars. How do clouds get their shapes? Clouds form when heated air rises. As it slowly cools, water vapor condenses to form a cloud. Clouds get their shapes when swirling air pushes them in different directions. Clouds really don't look like animals or people. It's just that we have fun trying to see shapes in clouds.

14

Why do people sink in quicksand?

Quicksand is just an ordinary mixture of sand and clay that becomes water-logged, reducing friction between the sand particles. Such a mushy mixture cannot support weight. Quicksand itself won't suck you down, but you can get stuck in it. Moving will cause you to sink deeper. But don't despair—quicksand is generally only a few feet deep. How do you get out of quicksand? The best thing to do is to move slowly. If you struggle, you'll sink. If you relax and try to lie on your back, you can get yourself out of this mess.

Why is soil mostly brown?

Sometimes soil is red, yellow, or even black. Most soil, however, is brown. Soil is created by the way plants and animals **decompose**. Over time, dead trees, flowers, and even bits of food break down, or rot. Organic material that decomposes leaves behind minerals. They give soil its color. Different colors show different minerals. Red soil, for example, is high in iron.

WHY DO SINKHOLES FORM?

When rock under the soil wears away, it can leave huge spaces underground. Suddenly, the soil collapses—a sinkhole is born. Sinkholes come in various sizes. They are mainly caused by water circulating underground that dissolves the surrounding rock. Some sinkholes are big enough to swallow up entire buildings.

15

Why do flags **wave** and tree branches **sway?**

Look outside. Can you see tree branches moving or a flag waving? If so, the wind is blowing. Wind is moving air formed by pressure differences in the atmosphere. **Air pressure** is caused by differences in temperature. Warm temperatures expand air molecules, causing air to weigh less and creating low air pressure. Cold temperatures press air molecules together, causing high air pressure. Wind begins to blow when air molecules flow from high pressure areas to low pressure areas.

HOW CAN IT BE 8 A.M. IN NEW YORK WHEN IT'S 2 P.M. IN FRANCE?

Welcome to the wonderful world of time zones. Humans created time zones—a uniform standard of time—because of Earth's rotation. Only one section of the globe faces the sun at any given time. As one side of Earth has daylight, the other side of the planet is having nighttime. There are 24 times zones because it takes Earth 24 hours to make one complete turn on its axis.

Why is it **winter** in Detroit, Michigan, while it's **summer** in Sydney, Australia?

Because Detroit is in the Northern Hemisphere, and Sydney is in the Southern Hemisphere, the seasons are reversed. Why is that? Earth tilts on its axis as it moves around the sun. When it's wintertime in Detroit, or anywhere else in the Northern Hemisphere, Earth is tilted away from the sun. So, the sun's rays indirectly strike the Northern Hemisphere, causing winter conditions. At the same time, Australia and the rest of the Southern Hemisphere are tilted more toward the sun. The sun's rays strike the Southern Hemisphere more directly, resulting in summer conditions.

The colors in this satellite photo show different hurricane wind speeds near Florida.

Why are hurricane winds so powerful?

The wind from a hurricane can rip buildings from their foundations and knock trees down. Hurricanes have winds that blow at least 74 miles (119.09 km) per hour. Hurricanes are fueled by warm ocean water. When a storm passes over warm water, the strong rotational movement of Earth causes the moist air over the ocean to spiral upward. As the air rises, it cools and falls as rain. The heat given off when the air condenses creates huge amounts of energy, causing a hurricane to form.

WHY CAN'T SCIENTISTS STOP HURRICANES?

Hurricanes are so massive that they are impossible to stop or weaken. During the 1960s, the National Oceanic and Atmospheric Administration (NOAA) tried various ways to weaken hurricanes, but it could not stop the huge storms.

WHY WAS HURRICANE KATRINA SO DEADLY?

When Hurricane Katrina passed over the Gulf Coast in 2005, the storm killed many people. Most of the deaths were in New Orleans, where a **storm surge**—a massive wall of water—overwhelmed the city's **levees,** which are supposed to hold back water from Lake Pontchartrain and the Mississippi River. New Orleans, which lies below sea level, flooded. At least 1,836 people died during the storm, and entire neighborhoods along the Gulf Coast were destroyed.

Why is Mount Everest so tall?

Some 250 million years ago, India, Africa, Australia, and South America were all one continent that scientists call Pangea. About 60 million years ago, the tectonic plate that India sits on moved northward, charging across the equator at roughly 5.91 inches (15 cm) a year. Eventually, India slammed into Asia. The collision erased an ocean named the Tethys Sea. The colliding plates and the sinking ocean floor pushed up the Himalaya Mountains, including what became Mount Everest, the tallest mountain in the world.

Why are Earth's ice caps melting?

The heat is on in Antarctica and the Arctic. Global warming, an overall rise in Earth's temperature, is melting the polar ice caps. The rise in temperatures is causing huge chunks of Antarctic ice to fall into the ocean. In the Arctic, polar bears are finding their icy territories melting, causing the beautiful bears to be endangered.

WHY ARE THE HIGHEST MOUNTAINS NEAR THE EQUATOR?

Mountains form when tectonic plates slam into one another. That force, coupled with **erosion**, determines the height of mountain ranges. Scientists say **glaciers** play a major role, too. The closer a mountain is to Earth's poles, the easier it is for glaciers to cut mountains down to size. Peaks are higher near the equator because glaciers don't impact the mountains there as much.

Why does Earth have different types of rocks?

Earth rocks! While there are many different types of rocks on the planet, they fall into only three categories: igneous, metamorphic, and sedimentary.

- Igneous rocks, such as pumice, form when molten rock reaches Earth's surface and cools.
- Metamorphic rocks, such as marble, are created when heat and pressure bind different rocks together.
- Sedimentary rocks, such as limestone, form when sediment builds up and is compacted.

Metamorphic Rock

Sedimentary Rock

Igneous Rock

WHY ARE SOME ROCKS HARDER THAN OTHERS?

Rocks are made from minerals. The harder the minerals, the harder the rock will be. Diamonds are the hardest rocks on the planet, talc the softest.

Why are diamonds so rare?

Diamonds form when carbon deep below Earth's surface is squeezed under tremendous pressure. Diamonds are uncommon because pressure seldom pushes the gems to the surface. In fact, only 350 tons (317,515 kg) of diamonds have ever been mined.

19

Why are planets round?

People once thought Earth was flat. Then someone figured out that Earth and the other planets were round. Planets are round due to gravity's pull. As planets form, **gravity** pulls **matter** inward toward the center of the planet. When that happens, every part of the planet is pulled evenly toward the center, giving the planet its spherical shape. Planets are not perfectly round, however. Because Earth is spinning, centrifugal force causes the planet to have a slight bulge in its mid-section.

WHY DO STARS TWINKLE?

Stars really don't twinkle. It just looks that way. Stars appear to twinkle because we view them through thick layers of hot and cool air in Earth's atmosphere. Since the air is moving, the light of the star bends as it travels through the atmosphere. Each time you look at the star, the path of its light has changed slightly, giving the illusion that it twinkles.

Why are stars invisible during the day?

If you live in Hollywood, you see stars all the time—even during the day. However, most people see only one star during daylight hours—our sun. The sun's brightness during the day blocks out the light from other stars.

WHY DO SCIENTISTS STUDY COMETS?

Many scientists say comet dust contains the building blocks of planets, including carbon, hydrogen, and oxygen. These are some of the elements that went into forming Earth 4 billion years ago. NASA—the U.S. space agency—even sent a space probe to bring back a bit of comet dust for study. When the probe, *Stardust* (right), returned to Earth, scientists discovered the ancient building blocks of the solar system that they were looking for.

WHY DO COMETS HAVE NAMES?

Comets are named for those who discovered them. In the late 1980s, about a dozen comets were discovered each year. Now, about 30 comets a year are found, because there are more people looking for them. Sometimes, comets have combined names, like Hale-Bopp. That's because more than one person discovered the comet.

Why do comets' tails look like they're on fire?

Comets are dirty snowballs—huge lumps of frozen water, carbon dioxide, methane, and ammonia. When a comet gets close to the sun, the heat of the sun causes the ice to melt, forming a long, dusty tail. When a comet moves away from the sun, its tail disappears.

Why is the sun so bright?

The sun is a big ball of super heated gas that generates as much energy every second as all t power plants on Earth could produce in about 2 million years! The sun gets its enormous energy through fusion, a nuclear reaction that joins together the **nuclei** of atoms. Fusion takes place deep inside the sun at temperatures of 27 milli (15 million°C). Fusion converts hydrogen to heli and releases energy, which makes the sun very bright and able to give off so much light and he

WHY DON'T PLANETS FLY OFF INTO SPACE?

The sun is gigantic–roughly 333,000 times the size of Earth! Something that big has a lot of mass and therefore a lot of gravity. The sun's gravitational pull, coupled with the sideways motion of the planets, is why the planets orbit the sun and why everything in the solar system doesn't crash into the sun or fly off into outer space.

Why does the sun have spots?

Sunspots are relatively cool areas on the sun's surface. Th spots are about 5,840°F (3,227°C). They are created whe strong **magnetic fields** rise from the sun's interior to the surface. These magnetic fields interrupt the normal proc that brings energy to the sun's surface and makes it brigh and hot. Sunspots are roughly 30,000 miles (48,000 km)

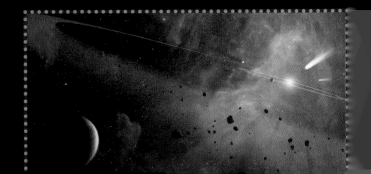

Why can I sometimes see the moon during the day?

You can see the moon during the day—and at night—because the sun's light is reflecting brilliantly off the moon's surface. In addition, the moon is close to Earth, only 238,000 miles (383,000 km) away, which makes it easier to see on some days.

Scientists found water on the moon in 2009.

WHY IS IT WE NEVER SEE THE OTHER SIDE OF THE MOON?

Every time you look at the moon do you notice something familiar? It always looks the same. Why is that? The moon and Earth are locked in **synchronous rotation**. In other words, it takes the same amount of time for the moon to orbit Earth as it takes for the moon to rotate on its axis. That means the same side of the moon faces Earth all the time.

Why does the moon appear to change its shape?

As the moon orbits Earth each month, Earth blocks sunlight from hitting the moon at different angles. As that happens, different portions of the moon are in shadow.

WHY IS THE MOON POCKMARKED WITH CRATERS?

Falling asteroids and meteorites created thousands of craters on the moon's surface. Unlike Earth, the moon does not have a protective atmosphere that destroys most meteors before they strike the ground.

23

Why do we call Mars the Red Planet?

We should really call Mars the Rusty Planet. Its soil is rich in iron oxides, known to Earthlings as rust. Iron oxides are chemical **compounds** made up of iron and oxygen that give off a reddish color. Some ancient people used to think that blood caused the reddish glow of Mars.

WHY WOULDN'T WE BE ABLE TO BREATHE ON MARS?

The atmosphere on Mars is made up mostly of carbon dioxide, a gas that trees on Earth love but is poisonous to humans.

Why are there canals on Mars?

Although many people used to think that Mars had canals, that's not the case. Giovanni Schiaparelli (jaw-VAHN-nee skyah-puh-REL-ee) first spotted straight lines on the planet's surface in 1877. He called those lines "*canali.*" In Italian, *canali* means channels or grooves. However, people mistakenly translated the word into English as "canals." Some people even claimed Martians built the "canals." When viewed from Earth with telescopes that have limited **resolution**, the canals are nothing more than optical illusions caused by craters and other surface features.

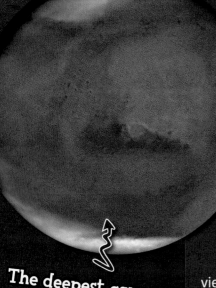

The deepest canyon on Mars is 4.35 miles (7 km) deep.

What is *Sputnik?*

Sputnik was Earth's first orbiting satellite. The Soviet Union launched *Sputnik* on October 4, 1957. The satellite traveled 18,000 miles (29,000 km) per hour. It took roughly 96 minutes to circle Earth. When *Sputnik* orbited the planet, it didn't do much—except beep. People could even watch it as it passed ove head. *Sputnik*'s launch touched off a race to the moon between the Soviet Union and the United States. *Sputnik* burned up in the atmosphere on January 4, 1958, as it fell from its orbit.

HAVE ANY RUSSIANS WALKED ON THE MOON?

Although the United States and the Soviet Union battled one another in the space race to the moon, only Americans have set foot on the moon. However, in 1959, the Soviet-built *Luna 2* was the first human-made spaceship to reach the lunar surface.

Sputnik was the world's first spacecraft.

Cuba, the Soviet Union's close friend, honored Tereshkova on a postage stamp.

WHO WAS THE FIRST WOMAN IN SPACE?

Valentina Vladimirovna Tereshkova was a Soviet cosmonaut and the first woman in space. On June 16, 1963, Tereshkova blasted into orbit and she circled Earth 48 times. Before becoming a cosmonaut, Tereshkova was a factory worker. The first American woman in space was Sally Ride, who rode into space on June 18, 1983, aboard *Challenger*.

How were planets formed?

Our solar system, and the entire universe for that matter, started with a big bang some 13.7 billion years ago! The explosion threw out a lot of dust and gas. The explosion released so much energy that it made the dust and gas mixture cook. Bits of dust banded together, making bigger clumps. As these clumps of dust got larger, gravity held them together. In time, one clump of gas began to generate its own energy, forming our sun. The remaining dust and gas came together and swirled around the new sun. Eventually these bits of dust and gas turned into the planets.

WHY DON'T PLANETS ORBIT IN PERFECT CIRCLES?

Planets revolve around the sun in **elliptical**, or oval-like orbits, also known as eccentric orbits. The sun's gravitational pull tugs the planets one way, while the other planets tug each other in other ways. This planetary tug-of-war, along with the speed and time it takes a planet to orbit the sun, causes an eccentric orbit.

Did people once believe the sun revolved around Earth?

Everyone from the ancient Greeks up through people living in the Middle Ages, which lasted from around 400 to 1500 A.D., believed Earth was the center of the universe. They believed the sun, the moon, and the planets revolved around Earth. In 1543, an astronomer named Nicolas Copernicus said the Earth and the planets revolved around the sun. In 1610, Galileo Galilei, an Italian astronomer, used a telescope to prove that Copernicus was right.

Why aren't all planets rocky like Earth?

When the solar system first began to form, some of the dust from an exploding star joined together to form planets. Because it was so cold in the outer reaches of the solar system, some of the gas and dust froze into huge gas balls such as Jupiter and Saturn. Planets closer to the sun, such as Earth and Mars, turned into big chunks of rock.

WHY ARE THE RINGED PLANETS NEAR EACH OTHER?

Jupiter, Saturn, and Neptune have so much mass and so much gravity that they are able to hold on to their rings. If these planets were closer to the sun, like the Earth, Venus, and Mercury, the sun's gravitational pull would have shredded these rings to pieces.

Why do some planets have rings?

Some planets act like a catcher's mitt. When small moons and comets get too close to a planet, gravity rips them apart. Bits of rock and ice begin orbiting the planet, eventually forming rings.

Saturn has a ring that can hold 1 billion Earths.

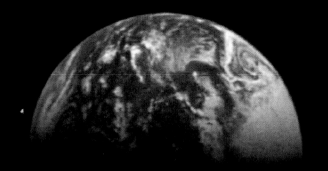

Why does Earth have a moon?

Scientists have scratched their heads for centuries trying to figure out where the moon came from. They believe an object about the size of Mars slammed into Earth a long time ago. That crash sent a huge chunk of Earth into outer space where it began orbiting the planet as our moon. Earth's gravitational pull keeps the moon in place.

Did Earth ever have **more than one moon?**

In the early 1980s, two scientists came up with a theory in which they said Earth once had many moons. According to this theory, Earth was struck by some huge object, sending hundreds, if not thousands, of smaller objects into space. These "moonlets" lingered between the moon and Earth for 100 million years. Then, Earth's orbit suddenly shifted. When that happened, the moonlets drifted away or crashed onto the surfaces of the moon and Earth.

WHY DID PEOPLE ONCE THINK THERE WERE SEAS ON THE MOON?

Long before telescopes and spaceships, humans viewed the moon with naked eyes. They couldn't see mountains or valleys, but they did see huge areas that they believed were seas—just like on Earth. We still call these areas seas, although they are not wet.

Why is Pluto no longer considered a planet?

A planet is an object that orbits the sun with enough mass to allow gravity to form a round shape. Once upon a time, Pluto was the smallest, coldest, and least understood planet in the solar system. Many people said Pluto shouldn't be called a planet at all. They said Pluto was too small and basically just a chunk of ice, like many other objects in the Kuiper Belt, a disk-shaped region beyond the orbit of Neptune. In 2006, the International Astronomical Union formally downgraded Pluto to a dwarf planet, which is smaller than a regular planet.

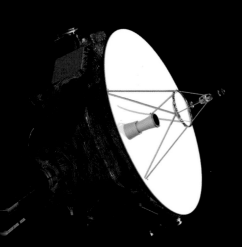

How long would it take a spacecraft to reach Pluto?

Pluto is roughly 2.9 billion miles from the sun. Pluto is so far away that a spacecraft would need about nine years to reach the planet from Earth. In January 2006, NASA launched the first mission to Pluto, called *New Horizons*. The unmanned spacecraft will reach its closest encounter with Pluto in July 2015. On February 25, 2010, *New Horizons* reached the half-way point between Earth and Pluto.

WHY DO HUMANS WEIGH LESS ON THE MOON THAN ON EARTH?

Since the moon is much smaller than Earth, its force of gravity is less. Gravity on the moon is about one-sixth as strong as gravity on Earth. So, humans weigh less on the moon than they do on Earth. For example, if you weigh 100 pounds (45.36 kg) on Earth, you would weigh about 16 pounds (7.6 kg) on the moon.

Why do stars form?

Stars are born in giant clouds of dust. Such clouds are scattered throughout the galaxy. Inside these clouds, gravity causes gas and dust to collapse. As that happens, the stuff in the center of the cloud heats up. The hot core at the heart of the collapsing cloud—known as a protostar—will one day become a star.

WILL THE SUN STOP SHINING SOMEDAY?

Yes, but not for at least 5 billion years. The sun is a ball of superheated gases, made up mostly of hydrogen, a small amount of helium, and very small amounts of other elements. The sun uses these gases to generate heat and light. In about 5 billion years the hydrogen in the sun will run out. When that happens, there won't be enough fuel for the sun to shine or give off heat.

Supernovas are billions of times brighter than our sun.

What is a supernova?

Stars are born. They live out their lives, and then they explode and die. As a star begins to explode, its core quickly collapses. As the core collapses, the star releases a whole lot of energy. Such a massive amount of energy causes the star to erupt into a supernova. A supernova will shine a billion times brighter than our sun before it fades from view.

Where does our solar system end?

Far beyond Neptune and Pluto is the boundary of our solar system, a place called the heliopause. The heliopause is where the sun's gravity has little effect. Beyond the heliopause lies deep space.

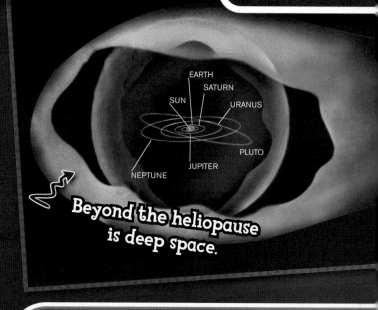

EARTH
SATURN
SUN
URANUS
PLUTO
JUPITER
NEPTUNE

Beyond the heliopause is deep space.

WHY CAN'T WE BREATHE IN SPACE?

Gravity holds everything on Earth in place, including oxygen in the atmosphere. We need oxygen in every breath to stay alive. The Earth's atmosphere provides that so we can breathe. There are a lot of gases in space, and oxygen is one of them. Because there is so little gravity in space, there's nothing to hold the gases together to create any atmosphere. Whatever gas there is spreads out very quickly over great distances, making it impossible for us to breathe without a spacesuit.

We cannot count the number of galaxies in the universe.

WHY DON'T STARS LIGHT UP THE NIGHT SKY?

Since the universe is expanding, distant stars and galaxies are moving farther away from us all the time. As that distance increases, the amount of light energy reaching Earth from the stars decreases. The farther away a star is, the less bright it will look to us. However, we won't see the night sky get any darker as the universe expands. Why? The starlight we see today is the light that left the galaxies and stars billions of years ago. Because it takes so long for a star's light to reach Earth, it would take billions of years before we would see the light of the star dim.

31

Why is our **galaxy shaped** differently from other galaxies?

As galaxies get older, gravity and the **centrifugal force** of spinning gas change their shapes. Galaxies contain hundreds of billions of stars. Some galaxies are spiral-shaped, some are elliptical, and some are irregular in shape. Spiral galaxies, such as our Milky Way, look like pinwheels, with outstretched arms and a bulging center. Other galaxies are shaped like cigars or sombreros.

Why can't we see the center of the Milky Way?

Our solar system is on the edge of the Milky Way. We can see a fuzzy band of stars that make up a portion of the Milky Way, but we cannot see the center of the galaxy with our naked eyes. There are too many stars and too much gas in the way. However, special telescopes can "see" the center of the Milky Way.

WHAT GALAXIES CAN WE SEE WITHOUT TELESCOPES?

We can see two of the Milky Way's closest neighboring galaxies—known as the Magellanic Clouds—without the help of special instruments or telescopes. The Clouds appear in the Southern Hemisphere and are named after the 16th century explorer Ferdinand Magellan.

Why are **constellations** named as they are?

The ancient Greeks, Babylonians, and Egyptians were among the most avid stargazers. Each civilization named the 88 constellations, or groups of stars, for **mythological** beings. To these ancient people, some of the constellations resembled animals, people, or objects.

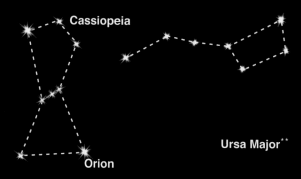

Ursa Minor**

Cassiopeia

Ursa Major**

Orion

*Constellation positions not in relation to one another.

**Shows only part of the constellation.

WHY DO THE CONSTELLATIONS MOVE ACROSS THE SKY?

It's not the constellations that are moving, but rather the Earth. Because Earth spins, we see the stars rise and set, just as we see the sun and moon rise and set.

WHY DOES THE NORTH STAR STAY IN THE SAME POSITION?

The North Star, or Polaris, sits directly above Earth's northern axis, so as Earth spins, Polaris does not move from its position. For centuries, sailors have used the North Star to navigate.

What is a shooting star?

When you wish on a shooting star, you're really wishing on a meteor. Meteors are small pieces of rock or dust that smack into Earth's atmosphere with such force that **friction** causes the falling debris to burn up in a fiery display.

Most meteors are the size of pebbles.

Why are asteroids different sizes?

Asteroids are chunks of rock and metal that orbit the sun. Asteroids play a cosmic game of football because they continually smack into one another. The collisions change their shapes and sizes. The largest asteroid is Ceres, which is 580 miles (933 km) long. The smallest asteroids are a few feet in size. Some are small particles loosely bound together. Others are small pieces of solid rock.

WHAT IS THE ASTEROID BELT?

The Asteroid Belt contains hundreds of thousands of asteroids. It lies between the orbits of Jupiter and Mars. People once thought the belt formed when a planet exploded. Now, most scientists believe asteroids are bits of rock that tried to form into a planet, but never did.

Why do astronomers measure **distances** in **light years?**

Since outer space is so vast, astronomers measure distance in light years rather than miles or kilometers. A light year is the distance light travels (in a vacuum) in one year—roughly 5.88 trillion miles (9.46 trillion km).

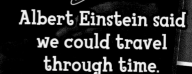

Albert Einstein said we could travel through time.

Why can't we travel at the **speed of light?**

If the car of the future could travel at the speed of light, it would move 186,000 miles (300,000 km) per second, or 670 million miles (1,079 million km) per hour. At that speed you would get to the moon in 1.2 seconds. However, Albert Einstein proved that only light can travel that fast, because of the laws of physics.

How do microwave ovens cook food?

You're late for school. Pop a toaster cake in the microwave, push some buttons, and within seconds you can have a fast and easy breakfast. Microwave ovens can heat food in seconds and cook meals in minutes. Inside the microwave is a special tube called a magnetron that changes electricity into high frequency microwaves. Microwaves are a form of electromagnetic energy. Microwaves cause water and food molecules to vibrate very quickly. This creates friction that produces heat, which can cook or warm up food fast.

The first microwave oven went on sale in 1967.

WHY DO PEOPLE MICROWAVE SPONGES?

Heating a sponge in a microwave for two minutes can kill the bacteria that can settle on the sponge.

WHY CAN'T I USE A METAL CONTAINER IN A MICROWAVE?

Microwaves can heat the metal to the point where it can cause a fire or produce harmful gases.

Microwaves can kill bacteria on a sponge.

Why does an **airplane fly**?

"Success... Four flights...Longest 57 seconds...Inform press. Home for Christmas." Orville Wright sent this message to his father in December 1903. He and his brother, Wilbur, had become the first humans to fly in a gasoline-powered aircraft. The Wright brothers realized that as the propeller pulls the plane forward, air moves across the top of the wing faster than it moves below the wing. That causes less air pressure on top of the wing than below. This creates lift, which causes the plane to soar.

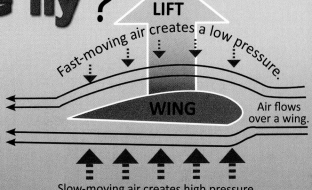

LIFT

Fast-moving air creates a low pressure.

WING

Air flows over a wing.

Slow-moving air creates high pressure that pushes upward, causing the lift necessary for flight.

Orville Wright was the first person to fly in a gasoline-powered airplane.

How does a jet airplane fly?

Jet engines combine air under immense pressure with fuel. When a spark ignites the mixture, it creates a jet of hot gases that escapes, producing forward movement called thrust. Once the jet is moving forward, the same principles that create lift in propeller-driven airplanes take over.

WHAT DO ROTORS ON A HELICOPTER DO?

On a helicopter, lift, or upward movement in the air, is produced by a copter's propellers called rotors. If a helicopter had only the large main rotor on top of the craft, it would spin in circles. A small rotor near the tail keeps the helicopter from whirling out of control. While airplanes can only fly horizontally, helicopters can move vertically and even hover in mid-air.

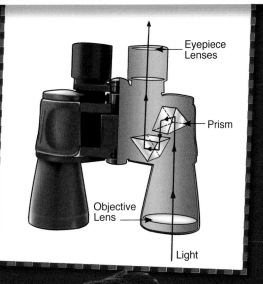

Eyepiece Lenses

Prism

Objective Lens

Light

Why do binoculars let me see faraway objects?

Binoculars are like a mini-telescope that people can hold in their hands. Inside binoculars are lenses that take in light from an object The lenses magnify the image. The light passing through the front lens and **prisms** then travels down the tubes and through lenses in the eyepieces, magnifying the image even further.

WHY CAN I SEE MY REFLECTION IN A MIRROR?

Most mirrors are made from glass and thin layers of aluminum or silver. You can see your reflection because light energy hits the smooth surface of a mirror and reflects back to you like a rubber ball bouncing off a wall. If the mirror is bumpy, light will bounce all over the place, and you won't be able to see your reflection as clearly.

WHY CAN I SEE THINGS THROUGH MICROSCOPES THAT ARE TOO SMALL TO SEE WITH JUST MY EYES?

The first microscope was built in 1590 by Hans and Zacharias Janssen.

Microscopes are super-powerful magnifying glasses that can make itsy-bitsy things easy to see. In an optical microscope, a light shines upward reflecting off the object being viewed. The reflected light passes through a special lens. That lens brings the object into focus inside the microscope's tube. The image is then magnified by a second lens in the eyepiece.

How does a lightbulb shine?

Every time you turn on a standard, run-of-the-mill light, something amazing happens. When you flick the switch, you are allowing electricity to flow. Inside a lightbulb is a thin coil of wire called a filament. The electricity flows through the filament, heating the wire to a temperature of more than 4,500°F (2,482°C). At such a high temperature, the filament glows, producing light. The glass bulb protects the filament and keeps oxygen away from the wire. If air were inside the bulb, the wire would burn very quickly. The glass also keeps gases such as argon and nitrogen inside the bulb, which allows the filament to last a long time.

HOW DOES A CANDLE BURN?

People have been lighting candles for centuries to find their way in the dark. When a person lights a candle with a match, the wick begins to burn. The flame slowly travels down the wick until it hits the wax. The flame's heat then begins to melt the wax surrounding the base of the wick. The liquid wax is drawn up to the tip of the wick inside the flame, providing fuel for the fire. The cycle repeats itself until all the wax is gone.

WHY ARE FIREWORKS COLORFUL?

"Ooh! Ahh! Ooh!" There's nothing like a fireworks display on the Fourth of July. Fireworks are colorful because they are packed with different chemicals. When these chemicals are lit, they burst into different colors. One type of chemical gives off a reddish color, while others produce green, white, and blue colors.

How did the first instant camera work?

Long before digital cameras, an inventor named Edwin Land created the first camera in 1947 that took instant pictures. It was called the Polaroid. Polaroid cameras worked just like ordinary film cameras, with one huge difference: the picture developed itself. The picture in a Polaroid camera contained layers of chemicals. Some of the chemicals were sensitive to blue, green, and red light. When a person snapped a picture with a Polaroid camera, the camera captured the image on a layer of silver. As the camera spit out the picture between two rollers, chemicals on the paper reacted with one another, allowing an image to appear on the layer of silver.

Polaroid cameras developed a picture almost immediately

WHY DO CAMERAS NEED A FLASH WHEN TAKING PICTURES IN THE DARK?

A camera needs light to capture an image. When it's dim or dark, a light flashing for a brief second throws enough light over the area so the camera can snap the photo.

You need light to snap a photo.

Why do people in photographs sometimes have red eyes?

If a subject is close to a camera lens, the burst of light from the camera's flash goes through to the back of the subject's eyeball. The **retina** inside the eye is rich in red blood vessels. When the light strikes those red blood vessels, it reflects the red color seen in the picture.

Why did **Alexander Graham Bell invent the telephone?**

"Mr. Watson, come here! I want to see you." Those nine words made Alexander Graham Bell famous. They were the first words spoken on a telephone. Bell didn't set out to invent the telephone. He was looking for a way to create a better telegraph machine. On March 10, 1876, Bell and his assistant, Thomas A. Watson, were working on what would become the first telephone. "I ... shouted into [the mouthpiece] ... 'Mr. Watson—come here—I want to see you.' To my delight he came and declared that he had heard and understood what I said." Bell later told his father that he could see the day when "friends converse with each other without leaving home."

In 1915, Bell places the first coast-to-coast telephone call.

HOW DOES A TELEGRAPH WORK?

Long before iPhones and smartphones, people communicated over long distances by using the telegraph. Invented by Samuel Morse and others, the telegraph let people send messages over an electrical wire. To spell out the words, a telegraph operator had to tap a transmitting key at one end of the line. A quick tap created a "dot." A long tap created a "dash." At the other end of the wire, a person listened to the dots and dashes and translated the coded message.

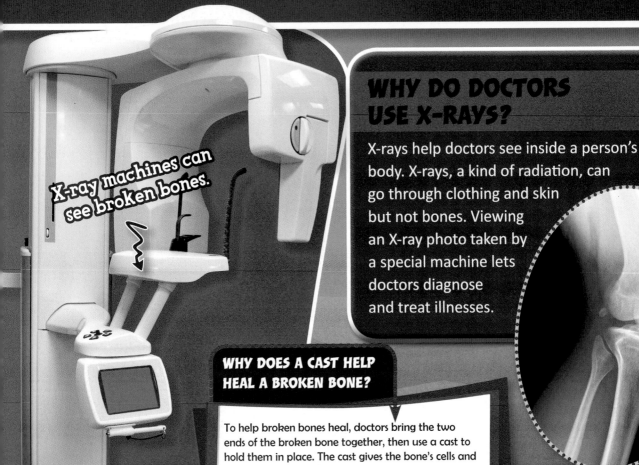

X-ray machines can see broken bones.

WHY DO DOCTORS USE X-RAYS?

X-rays help doctors see inside a person's body. X-rays, a kind of radiation, can go through clothing and skin but not bones. Viewing an X-ray photo taken by a special machine lets doctors diagnose and treat illnesses.

WHY DOES A CAST HELP HEAL A BROKEN BONE?

To help broken bones heal, doctors bring the two ends of the broken bone together, then use a cast to hold them in place. The cast gives the bone's cells and tissues time to mend.

How do vaccines work?

Vaccines are used to stop the spread of contagious diseases by making a person immune to a particular disease. Vaccines contain tiny bits of dead or weakened germs, which are not harmful. Those germs react with the body to make **antibodies**. Antibodies fight off disease germs that enter the body.

Gasoline is made from crude oil.

Why do cars and trucks need gasoline?

Gasoline is the stuff that powers most car and truck engines. When you put any amount of gasoline in a small place and light it, the fuel explodes, creating an enormous amount of energy. In a car engine, the force of that explosion causes the engine's pistons to move up and down. As that happens, the pistons turn a crankshaft that turns the tires on the car. Before you know it, you're traveling down the road.

Most monster truck tires are 66 inches (1,676 mm) high and 43 inches (1,092 mm) wide.

Why do some cars get **better** gas mileage than others?

Some cars can go farther on a gallon of gas than others. Why? Among other things, the engines of good gas mileage cars burn gasoline more efficiently than other cars. Also, cars get good gas mileage by moving at a steady speed, having properly inflated tires, and by having an engine that is in good working order.

WHY ARE TIRES MADE OF SEVERAL MATERIALS AND NOT JUST RUBBER?

Car tires are made from a combination of rubber, fabrics, and thin steel cables. The cables and fabric give the tire the strength and firmness it needs. Steel belts are especially important to make sure the tire doesn't puncture easily. The steel also helps the bottom of the tire stay flat on the road's surface so it moves smoothly. The grooved rubber on the tire's outside is called the tread.

43

Pencils contain graphite.

Why is there no lead in a lead pencil?

"Lead pencils" got their name when someone in 16th century England found shiny bits of stone near the roots of a fallen tree. People started to call the flashy substance "blacklead." They soon found the mineral was good for writing. Blacklead was really graphite, a form of carbon. The first pencils, then, were sticks of natural graphite wrapped in string or a wooden tube. The term "blacklead pencil" was first used in 1565. Today, some pencils are made of charcoal and other materials.

WHY DOES AN ERASER ERASE?

How many times have you worn down your pencil eraser to the nub in math class? An eraser, which is a chunk of rubber, is able to remove your mistakes by picking up tiny pieces of graphite particles left on a piece of paper by a pencil. An eraser does its job because the molecules in the rubber are stickier than the molecules on the paper. So the graphite from the pencil sticks to the eraser. Of course, erasing is a messy job. You have to wipe away the bits of eraser that come off as you erase.

Molecules in an eraser are stickier than paper molecules.

What are **crayons made of?**

Crayons are made of pigments and paraffin wax—the same type of wax used on fruits and vegetables to make them shiny in the grocery store. The two are mixed together and poured into molds, which are then allowed to cool.

Crayons are colored wax.

WHY CAN YOU ERASE SOME INK FROM A SHEET OF PAPER?

Often you can't erase a mistake if you are writing with a pen—unless you use a pen with erasable ink. These pens use ink made out of rubber cement. The rubber makes it easier to wipe away a mistake. However, within 10 hours, the ink will dry and harden on the paper so you won't be able to erase anymore.

How are colored pencils made?

Colored pencils are a combination of several ingredients: extenders (the body of the "lead"), binders, which hold the ingredients together, and pigments, which give the pencils their color. The ingredients are mixed together with hot water to form a paste. The paste is then rolled into sheets and pressed into long cylinders. A machine forces the paste through a small tube and cuts it into thin layers. Once the paste dries, it is sandwiched between two pieces of wood and cut into individual pencils.

FURTHER READING

Web sites

Animals
The Animal Planet's http://animal.discovery.com/ is neat. There are games, videos, and blogs.

Earth
Take a wonderful journey across the globe with this Web site from the Smithsonian Institution: http://www.mnh.si.edu/earth/main_frames.html.

Space
NASA's Web sites are out of this world. Check out http://solarsystem.nasa.gov/planets/index.cfm and learn more about our solar system. Click on a planet and discover amazing facts.

Humans
Go to http://kidshealth.org/kid/htbw/htbw_main_page.html and learn how the human body works.

People and Places
Explore the world on http://www.nationalgeographic.com/. This amazing Web site links to parts of the world many people don't know about. You can access news features, maps, and videos and learn about many different people and places. For the latest news about people and places, go to timeforkids.com.

History
If you're a history buff, go to http://www.history.com/. Click on "This Day in History" to find out what happened on any particular day. Learn about world leaders and play dozens of games.

Science
Read more about the world of science with National Geographic at http://science.nationalgeographic.com/science/.

Technology
If you're interested in some of the dumbest inventions ever produced, the editors of *Life* magazine have put them all together for you at http://www.life.com/image/3270485/in-gallery/25371.

Arts and Culture
If you're interested in the art of the Renaissance, http://www.renaissanceconnection.org/home.html is a wonderful place to learn about how Renaissance artists lived and worked.

Sports
Sports and kids go together like, well, sports and kids. Keep up with all the news of sports and play some games at http://www.sikids.com/.

Book List

Animals
National Geographic Encyclopedia of Animals by Karen McGhee & George McKay, PhD (National Geographic Society, 2006)

Earth
Smithsonian Earth by James F. Luhr (Dorling Kindersley Publishing, 2007)

Space
Smithsonian Atlas of Space Exploration by Roger D. Launius & Andrew K. Johnston (Smithsonian Institution, 2009)

Humans
Human Body: An Interactive Guide to the Inner Workings of the Body (Barron's Educational Series, 2008)

People and Places
History of the World: People, Places, and Ideas by Henry Billing (Steck-Vaughn Company, 2003)

History
Children's Encyclopedia of American History by David C. King (Smithsonian Institution, 2003)

Science
The Science Book: Everything You Need to Know About the World and How It Works by Marshall Brain (National Geographic, 2008)

Technology
Computers and Technology by Tara Koellhoffer, (Editor) & Emily Sohn (Forward) (Chelsea Clubhouse, 2006)

Arts and Culture
Performing Arts (Culture Encyclopedia) by Antony Mason (Mason Crest Publishers, 2002)

Sports
The Greatest Moments in Sports by Len Berman (Sourcebooks, 2009)

air pressure the weight of the atmosphere that pushes down on people and objects

antibodies proteins in the body that fight off disease and infection

centrifugal force the force directed away from the center of a revolving body

compounds the combination of two or more elements

decompose the process by which a dead organism rots away

dehydration the process by which a body loses more fluids than it takes in

elliptical egg-shaped

epicenter the point on Earth's surface that lies directly above the focus of an earthquake

erosion the gradual wearing down of soil

friction the force that one surface exerts on another when the two rub against each other

glaciers large masses of compacted snow and ice

gravity the force of attraction between two objects

levees an embankment that helps protect against flooding

magnetic fields the lines of force surrounding the sun and the planets generated by electrical currents

magnitude total amount of energy released during an earthquake

mantle largest layer of Earth's interior between the crust and the core

matter anything that has mass and can be measured; There are three types of matter: solids, liquids, and gases.

mythological stories that lack a factual basis

nuclei (plural of nucleus) the positively charged central part of an atom

ozone layer a layer of the upper atmosphere that absorbs harmful ultraviolet radiation from the sun and keeps it from reaching Earth's surface

pistons metal cylinders that slide up and down in an engine

resolution the quality of detail in an image

retina light sensitive tissue located at the back of the eyeball

storm surge a rise of water created by high winds

synchronous rotation a term that describes how the moon (or any other orbiting body), takes as long to rotate on its axis as it does to make one orbit around another orbiting body (such as the Earth)

ultraviolet radiation electromagnetic radiation invisible to the human eye

INDEX